Made in United States
North Haven, CT
05 May 2022

18927626R00085